CRABS

ANIMALS WITHOUT BONES

Jason Cooper

Rourke Publications, Inc.
Vero Beach, Florida 32964

PHOTO CREDITS
© Lynn M. Stone: cover, title page, pages 4, 7, 8, 10, 21;
© Breck Kent: pages 12, 13, 17; © Alex Kerstitch: page 15;
© Frank Balthis: page 18

Library of Congress Cataloging-in-Publication Data
Cooper, Jason, 1942-
    Crabs / by Jason Cooper.
        p.   cm. — (Animals without bones)
    Includes index.
    Summary: A simple introduction to the physical characteristics,
life cycle, and habitat of various kinds of crabs.
    ISBN 0-86625-571-0
    1. Crabs—Juvenile literature. [1. Crabs.] I. Title.
II. Series: Cooper, Jason, 1942-   Animals without bones.
QL444.M33C668   1996
595.3'842—dc20   95-26008
                                                              CIP
                                                              AC
Printed in the USA

TABLE OF CONTENTS

CRABS

Crusty crabs are some of the most colorful and interesting animals of the sea and the seashore.

Crabs are lively creatures that hustle quickly across sandy beaches and ocean bottoms. They are well known for their hard shells and their strong, heavy claws.

Almost everyone has seen a crab or its empty shell at the seashore. Many people have eaten crabs, too!

The blue crab's hard shell and sharp claws help protect it from enemies

WHAT CRABS LOOK LIKE

Crabs have shells that are wider than they are long. Underneath the shell, a crab has three or four pairs of "walking legs."

Several **species** (SPEE sheez), or kinds, of crabs have large front claws. The little male fiddler crab has one front claw that weighs as much as the rest of him!

Crabs can be tiny — less than one-quarter of an inch wide — or quite large. Big spider crabs can be 12 feet across from claw tip to claw tip.

The male fiddler crab has one claw that weighs as much as the rest of him

KINDS OF CRABS

The "catalog of crabs" has more than 4,500 species. You may find several kinds around one seashore or salt marsh.

The best-known crabs in North America are mostly kinds that people eat — blue crabs, kings, snows, and Dungeness.

One of the most unusual crabs is the hermit. Hermit crabs don't have hard shells of their own, so they borrow the empty shells of snails.

This land hermit crab has borrowed a snail's shell for its home

THE CRAB FAMILY

Crabs and their cousins are boneless animals called **crustaceans** (krus TAY shunz).

Scientists know of nearly 50,000 kinds of crustaceans. Most of them live in or near the sea.

Crustaceans have hard shells and jointed legs. Lobsters and shrimps are crustaceans. Lobsters have strong shells. Shrimp have clear, lightweight shells.

Crawfish, also known as crawdads and crayfish, are crab cousins. Crawfish live in freshwater **habitats** (HAB uh tats), or homes.

The American lobster, a cousin of the crabs, has the hard shell and jointed legs of crustaceans

The spider crab is named for its long, spiked, spiderlike legs

This Thailand land crab is one of the most colorful crabs

WHERE CRABS LIVE

Although most crabs live in the sea, a few kinds live in strange places. Ghost crabs live in sandy burrows above the reach of the waves. Land crabs live in seaside trees!

Fiddler crabs dig their burrows in the mud of salt marshes. A few crabs even live in fresh water.

Almost all crabs, even land crabs, begin their lives in the sea.

The calico crab is a marine crab

BABY CRABS

Salt water crabs lay their eggs in shallow seas. Crabs hatch as tiny creatures called **larvas** (LAR vuhz). The crab larvas don't have shells. They don't look at all like their parents.

Larvas eat and grow until they change into adult crabs. When young land crabs become adults, they leave the sea. They will come back to the sea to lay their eggs.

Still not an adult, this young red crab in California is a "crabster"

HOW CRABS LIVE

Crabs spend part of their lives hiding and resting. Crabs spend time busily scurrying about for food, too. Land crabs, for example, usually hide during the day and hunt at night.

Crabs have a curious way of running. They run sideways!

Some crabs have legs that look like paddles. These crabs are good swimmers. Other crabs have spiderlike legs. They crawl over rocks, hustle over sand, or climb into trees.

Like a tiny fire engine, a sally lightfoot crab hustles across a rocky beach in Ecuador

PREDATOR AND PREY

Crabs eat many different kinds of foods. Crabs aren't fussy! Some crabs eat sea scraps, like dead fish.

Some crabs eat dead scraps, but also catch live **prey** (PRAY) with their claws. The **predator** (PRED uh tor) crabs grab fish, smaller crabs, and other **marine** (muh REEN), or sea, animals. Blue crabs of the Atlantic coast eat oysters.

A few crab species aren't meat-eaters. Instead, they munch seaweed and leaves.

Crabs are prey for many larger animals, especially fish and wading birds.

A crab can become prey for a larger predator, like this night heron in Florida

CRABS AND PEOPLE

Crabs are an important seafood for people. "Crabbers" are boats that catch crabs in cagelike traps baited with fish or meat.

Some people "fish" for crabs. They dip lines baited with chunks of meat into the sea.

More Atlantic blue crabs are caught to be sold as food than any other kind of crab in North America. Pacific coast crabbers catch big king and Dungeness crabs.

People handle crabs carefully. Like pliers, their claws can pinch and cut.

Glossary

crustacean (krus TAY shun) — a group of small, shelled creatures with boneless bodies in sections; lobsters, crabs, shrimp, and their cousins

habitat (HAB uh tat) — the special kind of place where an animal lives, such as the muddy soil of a *salt marsh*

larva (LAR vuh) — an early stage of life in some animals; the young animal does not look like the adult it will become

marine (muh REEN) — of or relating to the sea and salt water

predator (PRED uh tor) — an animal that kills other animals for food

prey (PRAY) — an animal that is killed by another animal for food

species (SPEE sheez) — within a group of closely-related animals, one certain kind, such as a *blue* crab

INDEX